FROM CHALLENGE TO CHAMPION

INSPIRING STORIES OF SOCCER GREATS

FROM CHALLENGE TO CHAMPION

INSPIRING STORIES OF SOCCER GREATS

12 UPLIFTING TALES FOR KIDS

Chris Navalta

Illustrated by Lorenzo Fornaciari

Z KIDS • NEW YORK

Z Kids
An imprint of Zeitgeist™
A division of Penguin Random House LLC
1745 Broadway, New York, NY 10019
zeitgeistpublishing.com
penguinrandomhouse.com

ISBN: 9798217150847
Ebook ISBN: 9798217150830

Printed in the United States of America
1st Printing

Illustrations by Lorenzo Fornaciari
Book design by Katy Brown
Author photograph © by Shomari Smith
Illustrator photograph © by Jacopo Mastrangelo
Edited by Ada Fung

The authorized representative in the EU for product safety and compliance is Penguin Random House Ireland, Morrison Chambers, 32 Nassau Street, Dublin D02 YH68, Ireland. https://eu-contact.penguin.ie

For all the underdogs out there.
Every great soccer player has missed a goal once. Keep kicking—nothing is impossible.

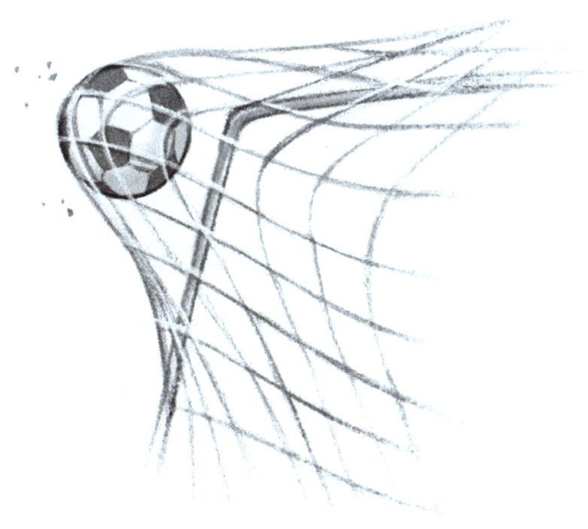

CONTENTS

HELLO, SOCCER FANS!

Hi! I'm Chris, and I love the game of soccer. I admit, there were other sports I enjoyed before soccer. But when I watched my first soccer game, I was immediately hooked.

My excitement for soccer grew even more during the 1994 World Cup, especially after watching the championship match between Brazil and Italy. After a scoreless tie at the end of regulation and overtime, it went to penalties. I remember Brazil's game-winning kick and how all the players rushed the field to celebrate. It was such an awesome moment, I'll never forget it.

During the 2006 World Cup in Germany, I could really see how much this game means to people. Seeing so many fans in the stands from all around the world showing their pride in their country, I felt proud for them, too! There's something about this game that brings people together.

It's easy to start playing soccer, but becoming a champion takes more. All you need to play is a ball, but some players didn't even have a ball, as you'll read in this book! You'll also read about a team that wasn't supposed to win many games but became league champions. Another great story will reveal the player who stopped growing as a child yet still became one of the greatest soccer stars of all time.

All because it started with a dream. Enjoy!

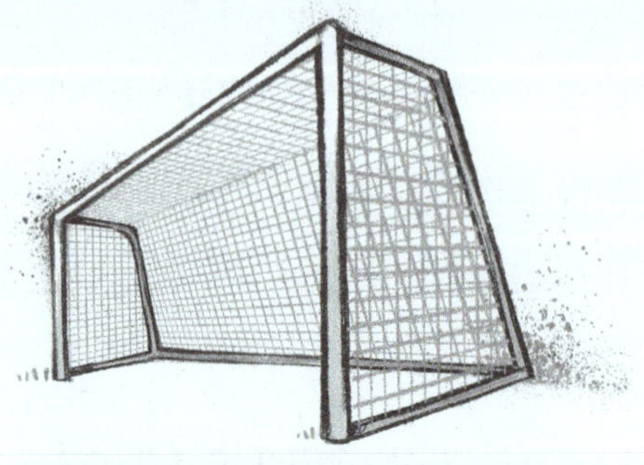

SOCCER WORDS TO KNOW

New to soccer (or what the rest of the world calls football)? Here's a list of words that will be helpful to know before you read these amazing stories. Flip back to these pages anytime you don't understand a word.

Game (or match): The typical soccer game or match consists of two 45-minute halves, with a 15-minute halftime break in between. This is known as regulation time. Each team has 11 players on the field—10 players and a goalkeeper.

Pitch: Another word for field. For example: "The two teams will meet at the pitch for their soccer match at noon."

Stoppage time (or injury time): Time added by the referees at the end of each half to make up for injuries, substitutions, or other interruptions that took away playing time during the game.

Clean sheet: When a team prevents their opponent from scoring any goals in a game. Examples can be a final score of 1-0, 5-0, or even 0-0.

Extra time: Additional time played when the score is tied at the end of the game and a winner needs to be determined. Extra time consists of two 15-minute halves, with a break in between.

Strikers: Also known as forwards, strikers play closest to the opponents' goal and are focused on scoring goals or assisting others with scoring goals. They often use speed and dribbling skills in their attack.

Wingers: Forwards who play near the left and right sidelines (or wings), typically on either side of the striker.

Defenders (or backs): Players who play closest to their own goal (besides the goalkeeper). They try to stop the other team from scoring. Center backs play in the center, in front of the goalie, and in between the left and right backs.

Midfielders: Players who play in the middle of their half of the pitch, behind the forwards and in front of the defenders. They move the ball forward for strikers and wingers and defend in front of the defenders. These players run a lot!

Goalkeeper (or keeper/goalie): The player who stands in front of their goal to try to stop the opponent from shooting the ball into the net. This is the only player who can use their hands.

Hat trick: Scoring three goals in one game.

Equalizer: A goal to tie the game.

Assist: The pass to a teammate right before they score. The player who makes that pass is awarded an assist.

Penalty kick: A free kick taken from the penalty spot, which is 12 yards from the goal. Awarded to a team after their opponent commits a foul, such as tripping a player or committing a hand ball (touching the ball with their hands).

Penalty shootout: How a game is decided if there's a tie at the end of extra time and there needs to be a winner. Five players from each team take a turn kicking from the penalty spot. The team that scores the most goals wins. If both teams make all five kicks, teams continue to take penalty kicks until one team makes a kick and the other team misses.

Club soccer: A competitive level of soccer, in which players on a team represent a city and compete in a league. Such leagues include the Premier League/Women's Super League (England), La Liga/Liga F (Spain), Serie A/Serie A Femminile (Italy), Ligue Un/Première Ligue (France), Bundesliga/Frauen-Bundesliga (Germany), and Major League Soccer/National Women's Soccer League (United States).

Tournament: A soccer competition that has multiple rounds, such as group play, round of 16, quarterfinals, semifinals, and championship. Tournaments include the World Cup, Olympics, and others.

Champions League: A tournament (one for men and one for women) where the best club teams from all the European leagues, including from the Premier League/Women's Super League, La Liga/Liga F, and Serie A/Serie A Femminile, play to determine the best of the best in Europe.

National team: A team made up of a country's best soccer players, who represent their country in international competition, such as the World Cup, Olympics, and others.

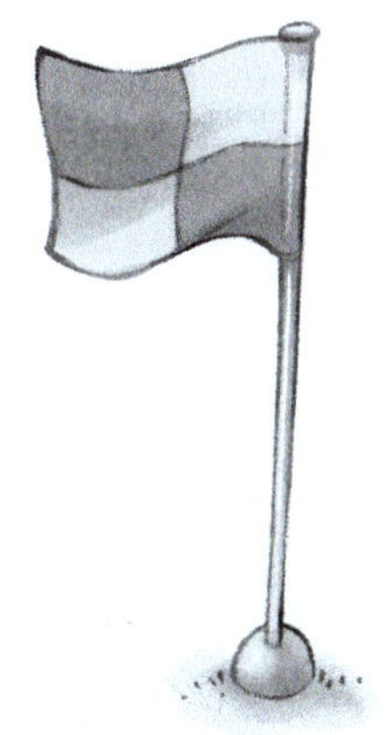

1999 US WOMEN'S NATIONAL TEAM

1

1999 US WOMEN'S NATIONAL TEAM

TEAM STARS

Michelle Akers
midfielder/striker

Brandi Chastain
defender/ midfielder

Julie Foudy
midfielder

Mia Hamm
striker

Carla Overbeck
defender

Kristine Lilly
midfielder/striker

Briana Scurry
goalkeeper

Tony DiCicco
coach

TOP ACHIEVEMENTS

- 1999 Women's World Cup champions
- 1999 *Sports Illustrated* Women of the Year
- 1999 Associated Press Team of the Year

CLUTCH PLAYS

- Briana Scurry's penalty save in the championship match against China was the only missed shot in the shootout between both teams and led to Team USA's victory.
- Brandi Chastain's game-winning penalty kick in the fifth round of the championship match shootout sealed the victory for the team. Her celebration afterward became one of the most iconic moments in sports history.

The 1999 US Women's National Team (USWNT) is one of the greatest women's soccer teams of all time. They might even be considered one of the greatest teams in any sport. Their Women's World Cup victory helped change how people view women in sports in America and around the world.

This team was not the first USWNT to win a World Cup. That was the 1991 team, in the first-ever Women's World Cup tournament. After that victory, many people thought more Americans would be interested in women's soccer. But when that team returned home from their victory, only three fans greeted them at the airport—and one of them was their bus driver!

In 1996, the USWNT won the gold medal in the Atlanta Olympics. That gave the team some momentum going into the 1999 World Cup, which was also going to be played in the US.

But would US Soccer, the official governing body of soccer in the United States, give the team the support it needed to play well? Would they help promote the team so fans would come and watch them play? Nope.

In fact, the US Women's National Team players were given just $10 a day by US Soccer for meals, hotel rooms, and transportation. To compare, the 1998 US Men's National Team players were given $100 a day during their World Cup.

The 1999 team also had to promote the Women's World Cup themselves. They had to use their own money to travel around the country to attend events, appear on talk shows, give interviews, and spread the word. However, the players were very smart, and they used their unique personalities to raise awareness for the World Cup.

As a result of all of their efforts and because they were the favorites to win, the

World Cup became a highly anticipated event. Women's World Cup president Marla Messing was amazed by how well the team promoted the tournament, so she requested that the matches be played in large stadiums instead of smaller fields. In her words, she wanted to "stage a breakthrough event for women's sports, and to inspire the next generation of female athletes."

Messing's plan worked—the USWNT made history even before the end of their first match. This game, against Denmark, in

front of 79,000 fans at then-Giants Stadium in New Jersey, set the world record for largest attendance at a women's sporting event. In front of the massive crowd, the USWNT went on to beat Denmark, 3–0. They followed that with a dominant 7–1 win over Nigeria, then a 3–0 shutout of North Korea.

Next came the knockout stage, where a loss meant elimination from the World Cup. With more pressure to keep winning, the USWNT faced Germany in Landover, Maryland, for the quarterfinal match. Germany was one of the best teams in the world—and the USWNT's biggest rival.

The game started badly. The USWNT went down 1–0 after defender Brandi Chastain tried to pass the ball to goalkeeper Briana Scurry. But the ball rolled past Scurry and into the Americans' own net.

"That could have been the worst moment," Chastain said about the play. But team captain Carla Overbeck told Chastain to let it go and keep believing that they would win the game. Soon, the USWNT tied the game on a Tiffeny Milbrett goal. The crowd got louder. But just before halftime, Germany scored another goal for a 2–1 lead.

"Don't let your dream end today," USWNT coach Tony DiCicco said to his team. "We can play better . . . we have to play better."

In the second half, Chastain made up for her mistake by scoring an equalizer, tying the score 2–2. Joy Fawcett followed with a go-ahead goal, and the US took the lead for good. This 3–2 victory sent the USWNT to the semifinals—just two wins away from a World Cup championship.

The USWNT won their semifinal match against Brazil, 2–0. More than 2.9 million homes in the US watched the match on TV, the largest cable audience for a soccer game—men's *or* women's!

The last test would be the World Cup final in Pasadena, California, against China. The US was favored to win, but China had defeated them in their past two meetings.

The match was so even that after regulation time, it was still scoreless. Extra time started without USWNT striker Michelle Akers, who had gotten hurt during regulation.

China's best chance to win was when Fan Yunjie shot a header that flew past Scurry. But defender Kristine Lilly was behind Scurry and saved the ball from going into the net.

DID YOU KNOW?

Members of the 1999 US Women's National Team packed good-luck charms with them. This included personal items like stuffed animals, rosaries, and photos of loved ones. Captain Carla Overbeck carried a lucky coin in her cleat bag.

Overtime also ended scoreless, bringing the game to a penalty shootout. Five players from each team would take turns trying to score against the opposing goalkeeper. Whichever team scored the most goals after every player had kicked would win the match—and the World Cup.

China was up first and made their penalty kick. 1-0 China. Next, Overbeck stepped up for the US. She scored as well. 1-1.

China's turn again. Scored. 2-1 to China. Fawcett took her turn for the US and scored. 2-2.

China took their turn. This time, Scurry saved the goal! Score still 2-2. Lilly's turn. She kicked and the US now led, 3-2.

China made their next kick and tied it up at 3-3. Now Mia Hamm's turn. She scored, making it 4-3 to the US. China's next penalty taker made her goal. 4-4.

It came down to Chastain. In a previous tournament, she had missed her penalty kick against China and the US lost. If Chastain made her kick, the score would be 5-4 and the US would win the World Cup.

Chastain stepped up and used her left foot instead of her usual right foot to make the kick.

This confused China's goalkeeper. Chastain scored—and the USWNT won the World Cup! Chastain ripped her jersey off, sank to her knees, and screamed with joy in a celebration that became known around the world and forever associated with the '99ers.

More than 90,000 people attended the Women's World Cup final. And more than 40 million people watched it on TV. It was the most-watched soccer match in American history until the Women's World Cup final between the USWNT and Japan in 2015.

The 1999 Women's World Cup victory influenced many future USWNT stars, including Alex Morgan (see her story on page 79), Tobin Heath, and Megan Rapinoe.

"That team was hugely influential," Rapinoe once said in an interview. "Growing up, my role models were more men. It was Michael Jordan, who we saw all the time, and there weren't many women on TV. So seeing the 1999 team excel with the whole country behind them was huge, and [it] was an incredible moment for the sport and these . . . athletes, who just happened to be women, igniting the entire country."

DAVID CLARKE

2

DAVID CLARKE

POSITION: Striker

BIRTH DATE: September 11, 1970

HOMETOWN: Wigan, England

TEAMS: England Men's Blind Football team, Great Britain five-a-side Paralympic team

BREAKOUT MOMENT: In a 2009 international match against Germany, David scored three times for a hat trick. The best part? The third goal became his 100th goal in international play.

TOP ACHIEVEMENTS

- Most international goals scored by any English player, visually impaired or not
- Member of the English Football Hall of Fame
- Three-time European Golden Boot winner

DID YOU KNOW?

As a child, David loved watching trains go by with his dad. His favorite kinds of trains were the Mallard and Flying Scotsman. Today, his kids also love trains.

What if I told you that one of the greatest soccer players in England's history is not only someone you might not have heard of but also his story is so hard to believe that it must be true?

Between 1995 and 2012, David Clarke scored 128 goals in 144 international matches—by far the most international goals by any English soccer player. He's a member of the English Football Hall of Fame and has earned the European Championship's Golden Boot (given to the tournament's highest goal scorer) three times.

He stands among the ranks of England's top players like Bobby Charlton, Wayne Rooney, and David Beckham, but his *story* stands out even more. Here's why: David is legally blind.

David remembers having eyesight and being able to see his sisters when he was just a year old. But a condition called congenital glaucoma caused his sight to quickly disappear.

By the time he was seven, he had completely lost his eyesight.

David did his best to live his life as normally as possible. Like many kids, David had a passion for sports. His parents were lifelong Liverpool fans, and at first, he followed soccer because his parents were fans. He started kicking the soccer ball around with his dad on the driveway. He discovered that soccer was something he wanted to play, and his parents supported him.

David attended a special school for blind children. There, one of his teachers created a special soccer ball for the students. The ball was filled with tiny ball bearings, which caused the ball to make a rattling sound as it rolled around. This type of ball helped the kids know where the ball was while playing on the field. This ball was an important first tool in David's soccer journey.

When he was 12, David moved to Worcester, England, to live at a boarding

school for the blind. There, he learned more about soccer and got to play competitively with other kids. Most of the other kids were older and bigger than him. Some kids were older than David by six years! They played on a regular-size soccer field, with the rattling soccer balls so players could hear where the ball was.

Sounds were important, but not just for the rattling ball. Players were also coached to speak up while playing. With practice, David got very good at hearing and responding to the different sounds on the field.

The more David played soccer, the better he got. But there were no organized soccer leagues for blind players and no coaches who could help blind players build their skills. This was frustrating for David. He really wanted to play competitively. Since he couldn't do that, he just played the game for fun and in smaller organized settings.

As David continued to play for fun, more blind people were beginning to play soccer, too. In fact, by 1994, there were so many players that an opportunity finally arrived: a new national team consisting of the top blind English soccer players!

This team, created by the Royal National College for the Blind, was led by coaches who knew about David's soccer skills. There was no question: He would be part of the team. In 1995, at age 25, David finally got to play competitive soccer, proudly representing his country.

Blind soccer is a bit different from how the game is typically played. Usually, teams play with 10 players plus a goalkeeper on each side, but blind soccer is played as five per side. In five-a-side, five players, including a goalkeeper who can see, start on each side. The field is also smaller than a traditional soccer field, and there are sideboards that allow the ball to bounce back into play. All players, except for the goalie, wear a blindfold so that they all have the same level of blindness.

In 1996, David made his international debut with Team England in a tournament in Madrid, Spain. Teams from France, Greece, and Spain also participated. His first goal was a penalty kick, marking the start of a remarkable international career.

The following year, Team England returned to Spain and competed in the Blind Football European Championship, where the team placed third. In 1998, David competed in his first Men's World Blind Football Championship tournament, where his team placed fifth. Then, in 1999, David and Team England reached the European Championship final. At the end of the tournament, he earned his first Golden Boot after scoring nine goals altogether.

David continued to show off his soccer skills against teams around the world. In 2008, he competed in his first Paralympic Games.

In 2012, when London played host to the Paralympics, David was named captain of his team. He even got to carry the Paralympic torch inside the stadium!

David retired from playing soccer in 2012, at age 42. By then, he was by far England's top goal scorer in the game. The following year, he was inducted into the English Football Hall of Fame and received a lifetime achievement award for his part in growing blind soccer.

Today, David is still very involved in sports. He is the chief executive of the British Paralympic Association, where he's responsible for England's participation in the Paralympic Games. He also tours around the world, sharing his life story to inspire others. You can always find him talking to kids who are visually impaired, encouraging them to get involved in sports because they can learn a lot from competition and teamwork.

As of 2025, 60 countries have blind soccer teams. It's the fastest-growing Paralympic sport since it officially became an event in 2004. While this popularity isn't all because of David, blind soccer wouldn't be where it is today without him. David's achievements showed that blind soccer is a highly competitive sport filled with skilled players, and it can be very exciting to watch.

David is grateful to those who helped him make this difference. “There were no pathways for people like me to play football for my local town or school—and definitely not for my country,” recalls David. “So, my parents and teachers played a fundamental role in helping me feel excited about playing the sport I love.”

GIANLUIGI "GIGI" BUFFON

3

GIANLUIGI "GIGI" BUFFON

POSITION: Goalkeeper

BIRTH DATE: January 28, 1978

HOMETOWN: Carrara, Italy

TEAMS: Parma, Juventus, Paris Saint-Germain

BREAKOUT MOMENT: In the 2006 World Cup final against France, Gigi stopped a header from France's top player during extra time with a fingertip save.

TOP ACHIEVEMENTS

- 2024 UEFA President's Award
- 2006 World Cup champion
- 2006 World Cup Yashin Award (now known as the Golden Glove Award)
- 10-time Serie A champion
- 13-time Serie A Goalkeeper of the Year
- Five-time IFFHS World's Best Goalkeeper

DID YOU KNOW?

Gigi comes from a family of athletes. His mom was a discus thrower, and his dad was an Italy junior champion in the shot put. His sisters played professional volleyball, and his cousin was a goalkeeper for AC Milan.

There may never be another goalie quite like Gianluigi Buffon, or "Gigi," as he is better known today. He played professionally for 28 years and became one of the top goalkeepers the game has ever seen.

Gigi fell in love with the sport when he was 12 years old, watching the 1990 World Cup. The tournament was held in Italy, his home country, but he couldn't stop watching Cameroonian goalie Thomas N'Kono. He was amazed by the saves Thomas was making, punching the ball away from the net. Gigi loved how bold and fearless Thomas was in his play. Gigi was determined to become the same type of goalkeeper.

In 1991, Gigi signed with pro soccer club Parma's youth academy. Just four years later, at age 17, he was called up to the senior team. But 1999 was his breakout year, where he helped the team win three major championships and earned his first Serie A Goalkeeper of the Year award.

In 2001, after six seasons with the Parma senior team, Gigi signed with Juventus. In his first season, Juventus gave up just 22 goals in 34 matches—the fewest in Serie A—thanks to Gigi. For his efforts, Gigi earned his second Serie A Goalkeeper of the Year award, and Juventus won the Serie A title.

Seems like Gigi had it all, right? If you were one of the best goalkeepers in all of soccer, with multiple championships and awards, wouldn't you be the happiest person in the world? It seems like a simple question with a simple answer. But being successful at a sport you love to play doesn't automatically bring joy and happiness.

Gigi knew this well. He was in the middle of a battle that nobody knew about. It was the toughest challenge of his career. One day in 2003, Gigi woke up with his legs shaking uncontrollably. The shakes were so bad, he couldn't even drive to practice. When he did practice, everything felt harder than usual. Suddenly, making a save became a really tough task.

At first, Gigi thought he was just tired and not getting enough sleep. But this went on for days. Then he thought that perhaps he was sick, and he just needed to sleep some more. But eventually, all he wanted to do was sleep and not do anything else, not even play soccer. He went to the doctor to see if it was something more serious.

After talking to his doctor about what he was going through, Gigi learned he was suffering from depression, a mental health condition that can include feeling sad or hopeless, or losing interest in things that used to bring you joy, for seemingly no reason at all. Gigi could relate—he was having these feelings.

By talking with a psychologist, Gigi realized that he'd been so focused on being a great goalkeeper that he hadn't spent much time exploring what he loved outside of the sport. He didn't have any hobbies or interests other than soccer.

One day, as Gigi walked past a local museum, he felt drawn to go inside. A painting by artist Marc Chagall caught his eye. The painting, called *The Promenade*, featured a man and a woman having a picnic in a park, with the woman flying in the air. It made Gigi smile.

As a result of that experience, Gigi developed a love for art, especially paintings that show what everyday life looks like. He realized that his world doesn't have to revolve around soccer—even as one of soccer's most talented and accomplished goalkeepers.

Gigi went on to play a total of 19 seasons with Juventus, getting better with every year. In Serie A, one of the top leagues in the world, it's tough enough to keep a clean sheet. Gigi did it 288 times! He was named Serie A's Goalkeeper of the Year a record 13 times—the most of any goalkeeper.

From 2001 to 2018, Juventus won four Coppa Italia championships, five Supercoppa Italiana titles, and nine Serie A crowns. The team made it to the finals of the 2017 Champions League, thanks to a string of clean sheets from Gigi, even against Lionel Messi's FC Barcelona.

Gigi's international career with Italy's national team was just as impressive. He served as a member of the team from 1997 to 2017—eight of those years as captain. His crowning moment came in the 2006 World Cup final.

With the game tied at 1-1 against France, French striker Zinedine Zidane (the team's

top player) headed the ball toward the Italian goal in extra time. Gigi leaped up, stretched his hand out, and tipped the ball over the top of the goal! His clutch save meant that the match ended in a tie.

The teams would settle the score in a tense penalty shootout. Both teams, along with 69,000 fans in attendance and over 715.1 million people around the world, watched in anticipation as Italy captured the World Cup! Gigi was named the tournament's best goalkeeper.

In 2023, Gigi retired as one of the most decorated goalkeepers in soccer history, winning 23 club championships—and, of course, one World Cup trophy. He also collected 506 total clean sheets, 77 of them while playing for the Italian national team, a team record.

Gigi speaks openly about his depression and the importance of taking care of your mental health. He finds talking about it empowering, not embarrassing. In a letter to his younger self in *The Players' Tribune*, Gigi wrote: "You cannot comprehend this now, at 17 years old, but I promise you that real courage is showing weakness and not being ashamed. You deserve the gift of life, Gigi. Just as everyone does. Remember this."

> If you think you may be suffering from depression or any kind of mental health challenge, please talk to a trusted grown-up about it. These issues are treatable, and there are many people who can help.

MARTA
10

4

MARTA

POSITION: Forward

BIRTH DATE: February 19, 1986

HOMETOWN: Dois Riachos, Alagoas, Brazil

TEAMS: Vasco da Gama, Santa Cruz, Umeå IK, Los Angeles Sol, Santos, FC Gold Pride, Western New York Flash, Tyresö, Rosengård, Orlando Pride

BREAKOUT MOMENT: In her Women's World Cup debut match in 2003, Marta scored her first goal in the opening match against South Korea. She was only 17!

TOP ACHIEVEMENTS

- Brazil's all-time scoring leader
- Six-time FIFA World Player of the Year
- Three-time Olympic silver medalist
- Four-time Copa América Femenina champion
- 2024 NWSL champion
- 2007 Women's World Cup Golden Boot

DID YOU KNOW?

Marta can speak four different languages (English, Spanish, Swedish, and Portuguese) and has dual citizenship in Brazil and Sweden. She also has a United States green card, which allows her to live and work in the US.

Like many Brazilian soccer players, Marta is known by just her first name. Considered one of the greatest soccer players of all time, Marta has set records like top Brazilian goal scorer and top goal scorer in World Cup history. Her achievements have inspired many girls around the world to play soccer.

While Marta is legendary in the women's soccer world today, she began her journey with nothing. No ball, no shoes—not even the support of some of her family members.

Marta lived in one of the poorest areas of Brazil, with a single mother who worked multiple jobs just to feed Marta and her three siblings. Marta watched her brothers play soccer, then began playing with them, too. Without extra money for soccer cleats or a ball, she played barefoot, with a ball made of plastic bags and old clothes. She was good! But her brothers didn't think she should be playing soccer.

In Brazil, soccer was viewed as a "man's sport," and girls were often told that they shouldn't play. People asked Marta's mom why she let her daughter play. Her mom ignored them and encouraged Marta to keep playing, but Marta was hurt by people's comments.

She was the only girl on her local team, and she felt lonely. In one tournament, the other team's coach declared, "This isn't a place for girls." He told the tournament's organizers that if his team had to play against Marta, he would pull them from the tournament. The organizers took his side and asked Marta to leave.

Marta cried at first. How could she be given the gift of remarkable soccer talent but nobody wanted to see her play? But then she decided she would keep playing, keep getting better, and prove everybody wrong.

When Marta was 14, her cousin helped connect her with a tryout in Rio de Janeiro with the women's club Vasco da Gama and encouraged her to go. This was a tough decision for Marta. It meant leaving her family and taking a bus for three days to get to Rio. And there was no guarantee she would make the team.

But Marta also knew that in Rio, a big city with women's teams, she might finally be accepted. She could show off her soccer talent and play with other girls who loved soccer as much as she did. So she bravely climbed on the bus and set off for Rio.

At her tryout, Marta finally had shoes to play in, an actual soccer ball, and green grass instead of flat, dusty fields. It was a whole new world for her!

Marta impressed the coaches right away. The first time she got the ball, she kicked it so hard that the goalkeeper fell back trying to stop it. The ball rolled into the goal—Marta scored! That was enough for her to make the

team. Marta was a professional soccer player at just 14 years old.

Marta played for Vasco for two seasons, followed by another two seasons with Santa Cruz, another Brazilian club. She then moved to Sweden to play for Umeå IK.

At first, the Swedish players at Umeå IK weren't used to Marta's creative, high-energy style of play, but her teammates soon embraced her. In her five seasons there, she became a club legend. In her first year, she helped the team win the 2004 UEFA Women's Cup championship.

And from 2005 to 2008, she led the team to four Swedish League championships in a row.

In 2009, Marta had the chance to show off her game in America, in the new Women's Professional Soccer league. There, she won a league championship with two teams—FC Gold Pride and Western New York Flash. She then played for two more teams in Sweden and even went back to Brazil to play club soccer. In 2017, she returned to America and joined the Orlando Pride in the National Women's Soccer League (NWSL). In 2024, she led them to the team's first-ever NWSL championship. Marta made her mark everywhere she played.

But Marta's biggest dream was to win a World Cup or Olympic gold with Brazil's national team. She'd lead Brazil to three Olympic silver medals. She played in a record six World Cups. She also scored a total of 17 World Cup goals—the record for any player, male or female. Marta even holds the Brazilian record for most goals scored of all time, with 122 goals!

One of her most memorable goals for the national team came during the 2007 Women's World Cup. In the semifinal against the US Women's National Team (USWNT), Marta scored after "nutmegging" a defender (dribbling the ball between the legs of her opponent and receiving it on the other side). Her brilliant goal helped Brazil beat the USWNT for the first time in a major tournament, but Brazil ended up losing to Germany in the final.

At the 2024 Olympics, Brazil fell short again, losing the final to the USWNT. Marta tearfully retired from international soccer. She was proud, even if she hadn't achieved her dream of an Olympic gold medal.

But in 2025, Brazil's coach persuaded her to come back for the Copa América Femenina, the top women's tournament in South America. Trailing in the final, Marta scored the equalizer to send the match to extra time. In the 105th minute, Marta scored the game-winning goal, giving Brazil a dramatic comeback victory! At age 39, Marta proved she could still be clutch.

Brazil is set to host the Women's World Cup in 2027. Will Marta play and give her ultimate dream another shot? With Marta, anything is possible.

As a six-time FIFA World Player of the Year, Marta continues to share her story about how she beat the odds and the doubters to become one of the best soccer players in the world.

Marta never forgot how she was treated when she was a young girl. She uses her platform to fight for other female athletes and give young female soccer players the opportunities she didn't have. Marta is an international hero—on and off the soccer pitch—to all women in sports.

5

LIONEL MESSI

POSITION: Forward

BIRTH DATE: June 24, 1987

HOMETOWN: Rosario, Argentina

TEAMS: Newell's Old Boys, FC Barcelona, Paris Saint-Germain, Inter Miami CF

BREAKOUT MOMENT: At just 19 years old, Messi scored all three goals in Barcelona's 3–3 draw against Real Madrid. His hat trick helped his team avoid defeat against their bitter rival.

TOP ACHIEVEMENTS

- Eight-time Ballon d'Or winner
- Four-time Champions League winner
- 10-time La Liga champion
- Six-time European Golden Boot winner
- Four-time FIFA World Player of the Year
- 2022 FIFA World Cup champion

DID YOU KNOW?

When he was younger, Messi ate pizza and drank soda before every match. Today he follows a more nutritious diet. His favorite food is his mom's chicken Milanesa.

It's not news that Lionel Messi is one of the greatest soccer players of all time. In fact, it's impossible to learn about "the beautiful game," as soccer is often called, without getting to know the player often known as just "Messi."

Messi has won multiple championships for his teams, individual awards for himself, and a World Cup for his home country of Argentina. But even though he has achieved great heights in his career, all that really mattered to Messi was just playing the game he loves so much.

Soccer is the most popular sport in Argentina, and Messi was born to love soccer. When he was just four, he joined Grandoli, a local club where his father coached. Even at a young age, Messi's talent stood out. His footwork and dribbling skills were incredible.

Messi was quick on his feet and could still control the ball. It was as if he was a character in a video game. His speed allowed him to easily go past defenders to score. Messi was so fast, it didn't matter how much older, bigger, or stronger the other players were. Soon other people noticed and began crowding around him to watch him play.

When Messi was seven, he went to play for Newell's Old Boys, his hometown youth club that he loved. His passion for the game continued to grow, along with his skills. But when he was 11 years old, he faced a challenge that nearly ended his soccer career before it even started.

Even though he played with other kids his age, Messi was always the shortest player. His family was worried that he wasn't growing very much, so they took him to see a doctor. He was diagnosed with growth hormone deficiency (GHD), which meant that he would not grow properly. Basically, Messi had stopped growing by the time he was 11.

The good news was that GHD could be treated with daily hormone injections. But the injections were expensive, and Messi's parents didn't make enough money to pay for the medication. Luckily, FC Barcelona wanted Messi on their team and offered to pay for his injections. It was decided that he would move to Spain and play for FC Barcelona's youth academy, La Masia.

Messi's first year in Barcelona with La Masia wasn't easy. He wasn't allowed to play much because of a disagreement with his old club, Newell's Old Boys. He also missed his mom, who had to move back to care for his siblings in Argentina while he stayed in Spain with his dad. Messi was also shy, so he didn't talk to his teammates much. In fact, some of them even thought he couldn't speak. On top of that, he still had to give himself injections every day.

Thankfully, Messi finished his medical treatment at 14, and he could now focus on the game he loved. After playing for the youth academy for the next three years, he made his official debut with FC Barcelona in 2004. At age 17, Messi was the youngest player to score a goal for the team. That year, the team won the La Liga championship. The following season, he won his first Champions League title with FC Barcelona after beating Arsenal in the final.

Though he didn't talk much, Messi let his game talk for him. His teammates loved playing with him, and his game inspired many of them to be better players. Teammate Xavi Hernández said, "Messi is an incredible leader, maybe quieter in the dressing room, but still an absolute leader. He's always asking for the ball, he's always making himself an option, he shows character. He's never hidden."

As Messi got older—and better—he evolved into a player who could attack the opponent in multiple ways. He still had the quickness and dribbling skills to blow by defenders, but he also learned how to use his vision and create plays for his teammates. Defending against Messi was really hard. His teammates were glad he was on *their* side!

During his time with FC Barcelona, Messi led his team to four Champions League titles and 10 La Liga championships. He also won an Olympic gold medal for Argentina in the 2008 Olympics.

Individually, Messi was named FIFA World Player of the Year four times and won the Ballon d'Or award, given to the best soccer player in the world, a record eight times. And as of 2025, Messi still holds the record for the most goals scored in La Liga—a whopping 474!

But there was still one championship that he wanted to win more than any other—the World Cup. The past two times Messi played in the World Cup, Argentina lost the final to Germany (2014) and was eliminated in the round of 16 by France (2018). But then came the 2022 World Cup. Messi was 35 years old, and there was a possibility that this would be his last chance to do it. The world was watching.

Messi scored a total of seven goals, including goals in every knockout game. In the championship game against France, he scored twice, winning his first World Cup and Argentina's first since 1986! Messi's win for his country put an exclamation point on his already spectacular career.

Today, Messi plays for Major League Soccer (MLS). When he joined Inter Miami CF in 2023, he immediately became the team's and league's most popular player. In 2024, Messi scored 20 goals for Inter Miami and won both the Golden Boot and the MLS MVP award.

Messi has created a legacy in the game. Many of his teammates through the years speak of his greatness, and say that they became better players because of him. Fellow star player Kylian Mbappé said it's easy to play with Messi because "he's the best player in the world."

As for the many kids who idolize Messi (maybe you're one of them?), you can find them on the pitch trying to dribble like him, or curve a free kick like him, or simply wearing his number 10 jersey.

But if you were to ask Messi what makes him special, his answer is pretty simple. "I just try to be myself and play the game the way I feel it. If that inspires people, that makes me happy."

2015–2016 LEICESTER CITY FOOTBALL CLUB

6

2015–2016 LEICESTER CITY FOOTBALL CLUB

TEAM STARS

Jamie Vardy
striker

Riyad Mahrez
right winger

N'Golo Kanté
defensive midfielder

Wes Morgan
center back

Kasper Schmeichel
goalkeeper

Robert Huth
center back

Leonardo Ulloa
striker

Claudio Ranieri
coach

TOP ACHIEVEMENTS

- Won the Premier League for the first time in team history
- Scored a team-record 81 points
- Had two separate clean sheet streaks—five in a row each
- Jamie Vardy, Riyad Mahrez, N'Golo Kanté, and Wes Morgan named to the Professional Footballers' Association (PFA) Premier League Team of the Year

CLUTCH PLAYS

- Down 2–0 late in a match against Aston Villa, Leicester City made a furious comeback, scoring three goals for the dramatic victory.
- Goalkeeper Kasper Schmeichel made a crucial save from close range for a 1–0 win over Crystal Palace. The win helped the team stay on top of the standings.

If there is ever an underdog soccer story, it's the story of the 2015-2016 Leicester City Football Club, also known as the Foxes. How did a little-known team in 20th place rise to win the Premier League, one of the best soccer leagues in the world?

To answer that question, let's go back to the previous season. The Foxes went through long stretches without winning any games. With nine games left, they were 20th in the league. If they didn't improve, they would be bumped out of the Premier League down to the less-competitive English Football League Championship.

But late in the season, the Foxes beat West Ham 2-1. That victory sparked a string of wins in what would become known as "the great escape." Leicester City ended the season in 14th place and earned their chance to play another season in the Premier League.

Okay, the Foxes showed they could win games—but the Premier League title? Not likely. Historically, that title was won by big clubs like Manchester United, Chelsea, Arsenal, and Manchester City. Before the 2015–2016 season started, fans and the media didn't think Leicester City would be very good.

Simply put, Leicester City was not supposed to be in the Premier League. They were given a dismal 5,000-to-1 chance to win the league title. What does that mean? Picture a large jar with 5,000 marbles. One of the marbles is gold, and the rest are white. Close your eyes and take a marble from the jar. What are the odds of you picking the gold marble? Close to zero, right? That's what people thought of Leicester City's chance of winning the Premier League!

The season started, and Leicester City won their season opener, 4–2, against Sunderland, with striker Jamie Vardy scoring one goal and right winger Riyad Mahrez scoring two. The Foxes won their next game and tied their third game. Leicester City was in second place in the Premier League! Although it was early in the season, many people were surprised to see the Foxes among the top teams.

Leicester City's first loss came in their seventh match, when they lost to Arsenal, 5–2. But they recovered and beat Norwich City in their next match, 2–1. The Foxes continued to pick up a draw or a win against Premier League opponents, keeping them secure in the top five in league standings.

But nine games in, the Foxes still did not have a single clean sheet. Coach Claudio Ranieri told his players that when they got their first clean sheet of the season, he would throw them a pizza party. This showed what Ranieri was like as a coach and how he motivated his players. He told them to have fun and believe in themselves, in each other—and in him.

The players were excited about the coach's promise. After all, who doesn't love pizza? Finally, in their 10th match, Leicester

City's goalkeeper Kasper Schmeichel and the defense, anchored by Wes Morgan and Robert Huth, got their first clean sheet against Crystal Palace. It was pizza time! The players celebrated as if they had won a championship.

Vardy scored the only goal for the Foxes in that match. He went on to score in the next three matches (all wins) to tie the Premier League's all-time record for most matches in a row with a goal scored. And in the next match—against Manchester United—Vardy scored again! He now held the record: 11 matches in a row with at least one goal scored.

Mahrez made big plays, too. In their 15th match, he scored his first hat trick in the team's 3–0 win over Swansea City. Leicester City hadn't lost in nearly three months, and by Christmas, they were on top of the Premier League standings for the first time in team history.

Something special was happening with Leicester City, and every team in the Premier League was now focused on beating them. The Foxes continued to stick together as a team. They kept picking up points in the standings with wins and draws. The more matches they won, the more fearless they became.

On February 6, Leicester City played second-place Manchester City. People predicted that this might be the start of Leicester City's downfall. But Huth scored for Leicester City in just the third minute, and the Foxes dominated the match and won 3–1. With that statement win, they showed everyone why *they* were the team to beat in the league. This team was captivating the entire soccer world.

By March, Leicester City was still on top of the Premier League. But Tottenham Hotspur wasn't too far behind. The Foxes knew that they needed to play strong defense—they couldn't afford to lose points the rest of the way.

So that's just what they did. The team that didn't get a clean sheet until their 10th match recorded five clean sheets in a row! What once felt impossible was now sitting on the horizon. They needed just three more wins.

But in their next match, the Foxes tied West Ham. And Vardy received two yellow cards (warnings) and was suspended for the next match. What would happen without the team's leading scorer?

For the next game, Coach Ranieri replaced Vardy with Leonardo Ulloa, who scored two goals in a 4–0 win over Swansea City! Leicester City had a chance to clinch the Premier League with a win over their next opponent, Manchester United.

DID YOU KNOW?

Jamie Vardy wore the same pair of shin pads and socks all season without ever washing them. It may sound gross, but Vardy believed they brought him good luck once he started his goal-scoring streak!

Unfortunately, that match ended in a 1-1 draw. But the next day—as the Foxes watched on TV—Tottenham Hotspur tied with Chelsea. There weren't enough games left for Tottenham Hotspur to catch up with Leicester City. So even though the Foxes weren't playing that day, they won their first Premier League championship in the team's 132-year history!

Vardy was named the Football Writers' Association (FWA) Footballer of the Year, as well as the Premier League's Player of the Season. Mahrez was named the Professional Footballers' Association's (PFA) Player of the Year. Vardy, Mahrez, Morgan, and defensive midfielder N'Golo Kanté were all named to the PFA Team of the Year.

This was a storybook ending for a team that started the season with no superstar players and a first-year coach. It took everyone on the team to win. Leicester City stuck together, and the players refused to let the doubters shake their confidence in themselves and in each other. When asked who his best player was, Coach Ranieri had a great answer: "The best player was the team."

Leicester City's Premier League victory is a moment in soccer history that will never be forgotten. They are proof that no matter how slim the odds—even 5,000 to 1—it's *never* impossible to become a champion.

ALEX MORGAN
13

7

ALEX MORGAN

POSITION: Striker

BIRTH DATE: July 2, 1989

HOMETOWN: Diamond Bar, California

TEAMS: Western New York Flash, Sound FC, Portland Thorns, Orlando Pride, Olympique Lyonnais, Tottenham Hotspur, San Diego Wave

---

BREAKOUT MOMENT: Alex scored a goal and assisted on another in the 2011 Women's World Cup final against Japan. She became the first woman to record a goal *and* an assist in a Women's World Cup final.

TOP ACHIEVEMENTS

- Two-time Women's World Cup champion
- 2016–2017 Women's Champions League winner
- 2013 NWSL champion
- 2012 Olympic gold medalist
- Three-time CONCACAF W champion
- Two-time US Soccer Female Athlete of the Year

DID YOU KNOW?

Alex wrote a bestselling children's book series called *The Kicks* that encourages young girls to play sports and follow their dreams.

Alex Morgan is one of the biggest names in soccer–and not just in the United States or in women's soccer. As an Olympic gold medalist and two-time Women's World Cup champion, Alex is adored by fans around the world because of her hard work and determination on the field, as well as her fight for equality for women off the field.

But long before winning championships and World Cups, Alex was once told that she wasn't good enough to be on a soccer team—by her own coach!

When she was six years old, Alex joined a recreational soccer team, which focuses on basic skills, teamwork, and having fun. At first, Alex just wanted to play for fun, but she quickly fell in love with the game. In fact, when she was seven, Alex wrote on a yellow sticky note: "Hi Mommy! My name is Alex and I am going to be a professional athlete for soccer!"

When Alex was 14 years old, she took the next step in achieving her dream, joining a club team. Many players start competitive soccer at a younger age than Alex did, but she wasn't scared. Alex wanted to challenge herself. But one of the coaches told Alex that her skills weren't good enough to compete and she would only be useful to the team as a practice player.

Alex always respected her coaches' feedback. Hearing that she wasn't good enough almost had her believing it herself. But this was just one person's opinion. And her dad reminded her that she could either choose to believe another person's opinion or she could believe in herself.

So instead of being upset or quitting, Alex used the coach's words as motivation to work harder and take her training more seriously. She joined a different club, Cypress Elite, where she had supportive coaches who believed she could become a great soccer player and compete at a high level. They were right!

Thanks to Cypress Elite and their belief in her, Alex became a three-time All-American in high school and qualified for the Olympic Development Program, a program for the top soccer players in the country. In her senior year of high school, Alex committed to playing college soccer at the University of California, Berkeley, her dream school. Around the same time, she was also called up to the under-20 US Women's National Team. Her future was bright! But then, misfortune struck.

Alex suffered a serious knee injury while playing soccer. But if she learned anything from when she was 14, it was to never let a challenge get in the way of chasing her dream. She was determined to come back and be an even better player.

Alex recovered just in time for her first year at college, where she led the team in goals scored. In fact, she would be her team's leading goal scorer all four years. She also led the team to the National Collegiate Athletic Association (NCAA) Division I tournament—college soccer's top tournament—every year. She did this while splitting her time with the US Women's National Team (USWNT).

The USWNT was where Alex shined the brightest. Her first major tournament with the team was the 2011 Women's World Cup. At 22 years old, Alex was the youngest player on the team. Although she wasn't a starter, she made history by becoming the first player ever to score a goal *and* get an assist in a World Cup final.

The following year, Alex started for the USWNT in the 2012 Olympics. The semifinal put them against Canada, the USWNT's biggest rival. This back-and-forth game went into extra time with the score tied at 3–3. The teams would play for 30 more minutes, plus any added time. If the score was still tied, the game would go to penalty kicks.

With only 30 seconds left in extra time, USWNT winger Heather O'Reilly kicked the ball from the side of the pitch toward the goal. Alex leaped high into the air and headed the ball into the net. The USWNT won! They went on to win the gold medal, and Alex ended the tournament with three goals and four assists.

In the 2015 World Cup, Alex was recovering from another knee injury. However, she played in all seven games, and scored in one, to help the USWNT win their first World Cup since 1999—and Alex's first ever.

Four years later, at the 2019 World Cup, Alex was now a team leader, both on and off the field. In the opening match against Thailand, she scored five goals along with three assists. And on her 30th birthday, Alex scored the eventual game-winning goal in the World Cup semifinal against England. She celebrated her goal by pretending to sip tea—striking a confident pose that has since become iconic.

The USWNT was dominating games on the field. They won the World Cup, and Alex received the Silver Boot as the tournament's second-highest scorer. But off the field, the team was in a battle with their own employer, US Soccer, over equal rights.

The USWNT accused US Soccer of gender discrimination, including less pay and poorer medical treatment and working and travel conditions, compared to the US Men's National Team. Alex was the team's voice, both in court and to the media. She explained what she and her teammates experienced and shared her frustration. In 2022, US Soccer agreed to pay $24 million to the USWNT players and promised equal pay from then on.

In 2021, Alex started TOGETHXR, a media company, with fellow Olympians Sue Bird, Chloe Kim, and Simone Manuel, to spotlight women in sports. And in 2023, Alex launched the Alex Morgan Foundation to support girls and women on and off the field.

Alex retired from playing soccer in 2024, but it's clear that her mission for gender equality and women's sports is far from over. Alex will continue to tell young girls to chase their dreams, no matter what—or who—tries to get in the way.

SADIO MANÉ &
MOHAMED "MO" SALAH

8

SADIO MANÉ & MOHAMED "MO" SALAH

MANÉ	SALAH
POSITION: Left winger	**POSITION:** Right winger
BIRTH DATE: April 10, 1992	**BIRTH DATE:** June 15, 1992
HOMETOWN Bambali, Senegal	**HOMETOWN** Nagrig, Basyoun, Egypt
TEAMS FC Metz, Red Bull Salzburg, Southampton, Liverpool, Bayern Munich, Al-Nassr	**TEAMS** Al Mokawloon, Basel, Chelsea, Fiorentina, Roma, Liverpool
TOP ACHIEVEMENTS ▪ 2019-2020 Premier League champion ▪ 2018-2019 Champions League winner ▪ 2019 Golden Boot winner ▪ 2021 Africa Cup of Nations champion ▪ Two-time African Footballer of the Year ▪ Senegal's all-time top scorer	***TOP ACHIEVEMENTS*** ▪ Two-time Premier League champion ▪ 2018-2019 Champions League winner ▪ Four-time Golden Boot winner ▪ Two-time African Footballer of the Year ▪ Leader in Premier League goals among African players

When Sadio Mané and Mohamed "Mo" Salah played together, it was like watching magic happen on the soccer pitch. Whether it was Sadio assisting Mo with a "no-look" pass or Mo finding Sadio through a sea of defenders, it seemed like they always knew where the other would be.

Together, they helped Liverpool win the Premier League, Champions League, FA Cup, and League Cup. But to get there, they both faced unbelievably difficult paths.

Sadio grew up in the poor, isolated village of Bambali, Senegal. He loved soccer as a kid and played barefoot on dry, dusty fields. Too poor to afford shoes or a ball, he played with a grapefruit, a can, or even rocks! He loved soccer so much, he dreamed of becoming a professional player. But his family didn't support his dream.

His father, who was an imam (an Islamic religious leader), thought Sadio should focus on school and religion. Although Sadio's father passed away when he was just seven, his mother and uncle were also against him playing the sport.

But when he was 15, Sadio took a risk. He left his family early one morning, borrowed money from a friend, and took a bus 250 miles to Senegal's capital city of Dakar. He hoped that his soccer skills would impress local scouts. But Sadio's old, worn-out soccer clothes didn't impress them. Many scouts rejected him, but Sadio didn't give up.

Finally, a scout from a local academy, Génération Foot, saw Sadio play and was interested in him. It was his lucky break. Sadio played for two years with Génération Foot, then joined FC Metz, a French club. Sadio's dream had come true. He was a professional soccer player!

Sadio kept getting better. After a year with FC Metz, he joined Austria's Red Bull Salzburg for two seasons before joining Southampton in the Premier League. In 2016, Sadio signed with Liverpool, where Mo would join him the following season.

Like Sadio, Mo loved soccer as a kid. In his hometown of Nagrig, Egypt, Mo spent hours playing with his brother and friends. He quickly became known across Egypt for his talent. In fact, soccer scouts traveled from Egypt's capital city of Cairo to watch him play.

Mo signed with his first professional club, Al Mokawloon, when he was just 14. It wasn't easy. He had to take several different buses and travel six hours a day just for practice! He quickly became one of the best players on the team. But in his second season, the Egyptian Football Association canceled the rest of the season.

At least Mo could still play as a member of Egypt's under-23 national team. In a friendly match against the Swiss club Basel, Mo was the best and fastest player on the pitch. He only played in the second half but still managed to score two goals. Basel signed him to a four-year contract soon after the game.

Mo played with Basel for two seasons, then moved to Chelsea—his first Premier League club. But he was often left out of the starting lineup.

This affected Mo's confidence. When he did play, he wasn't very effective. He later reflected, "I was like, 'OK, so now what? Are you going to be an average player or do you want to be a really good player?'"

DID YOU KNOW?

Sadio and Mo are both legendary for their generous charity work. Sadio helped fund his village's first hospital, along with a new school, post office, and soccer stadium, to name a few. Mo has donated millions of dollars to his village to provide clean drinking water, build a girls' school, repair a hospital, and much more.

He began reading and watching videos to get better. After two seasons, Mo left Chelsea to play in Italy, first with Fiorentina and then with Roma. Mo got the playing time he wanted and built back his confidence.

In 2017, Mo came back to the Premier League, where he teamed up with Sadio at Liverpool. Both Sadio and Mo had something to prove in their first season together. Fans and the press had called Sadio inconsistent. And Mo wanted to prove that he was a better player than he had been at Chelsea.

It usually takes new teammates time to get used to playing with each other. And there was some tension between them. But Sadio and Mo quickly became one of the best attacking duos in all of soccer. Mo set a record with 32 Premier League goals in his first season with Liverpool. That season, Liverpool finished in the top four in the Premier League.

They also made a remarkable run in the Champions League. Sadio scored 10 goals, including a hat trick, while Mo scored 11 goals with five assists. Liverpool eventually lost in the final against Real Madrid, but the best was still to come.

In the 2018-2019 Premier League season, Liverpool only lost one match. Sadio and Mo were so in sync that they scored the same number of goals each—22! The two teammates shared the Golden Boot, given to the top goal scorer in the league.

In the Champions League, Liverpool made it to the finals again. This time, Liverpool beat

Tottenham Hotspur, 2–0, winning their first Champions League in 14 years.

In 2020, with Mo and Sadio leading the way, Liverpool won their first Premier League title in 30 years! Together, Sadio and Mo helped Liverpool win six major trophies from 2017 to 2022. Mo assisted in 17 of Sadio's goals, and Sadio assisted in 15 of Mo's—a sign of true teamwork. Even though they were not best friends, Sadio and Mo respected each

CLUTCH PLAY

In a crucial Premier League match, Mo created space for Sadio by drawing his defenders away. This allowed Sadio to score on a dramatic late header in a 2–1 winner against Aston Villa. The victory kept Liverpool undefeated on their way to a Premier League championship.

other and knew they needed each other's teamwork to become top-level players.

But in 2021, the two teammates would have to play against each other in the final of the Africa Cup of Nations (AFCON). Sadio was the captain of Senegal, and Mo was the captain of Egypt. The game was a defensive battle. Neither team scored in regulation or extra time, so the game went to a penalty shootout.

Senegal was up 3–2 when Sadio stepped up to take his kick. If he scored, Senegal would win the AFCON title. Across the pitch was Mo, his longtime Liverpool teammate, but an opponent on this day. Mo was supposed to be Egypt's fifth kicker, but Sadio had other plans.

With the weight of his countrymen on his shoulders, Sadio stepped up and kicked his penalty low to the left, right past Egypt's keeper. Goal!

Senegal won the AFCON title for the first time in the country's history. It was a moment of pure joy for Sadio—and deep sadness for

Mo. It was bittersweet for Liverpool fans, watching one of their favorite players celebrate while the other suffered a tough defeat. After the game, Sadio wrapped an arm around Mo, consoling him.

As of 2025, Mo still plays for Liverpool, but Sadio now plays for Al-Nassr in the Saudi Pro League. They may no longer be teammates, but they're forever linked in Liverpool's history, no matter where they play.

MANÉ
10
10

CHRISTIAN PULISIC

9

CHRISTIAN PULISIC

POSITION: Winger/attacking midfielder

BIRTH DATE: September 18, 1998

HOMETOWN: Hershey, Pennsylvania

TEAMS: Borussia Dortmund, Chelsea, AC Milan

BREAKOUT MOMENT: In 2019, Christian scored a "perfect hat trick" while playing for Chelsea in a 4–2 victory over Burnley. (Read on to learn what a perfect hat trick is!)

TOP ACHIEVEMENTS

- 2021 Champions League winner
- 2019 CONCACAF Gold Cup Best Young Player
- 2017 DFB-Pokal (German Cup) champion
- Three-time CONCACAF Nations League champion
- Four-time US Soccer Male Athlete of the Year

DID YOU KNOW?

When he's not playing soccer, Christian also enjoys playing golf and chess. He even played against the world's top-ranked chess player, Magnus Carlsen, but lost.

There are two ways to earn the nickname "Captain America." One way is to be a comic book superhero and protect people from the forces of evil. Or you can be one of the best American soccer players in the world, like Christian Pulisic.

Christian grew up in Hershey, Pennsylvania (yes, the same city that makes the world-famous chocolate bar!). Both of his parents played soccer in college, and Christian fell in love with the sport, too. When he was eight years old, he answered an "All About Me" survey in class:

What do you want to be when you grow up? *"A pro soccer player."*

What do you like to do the most? *"Play soccer."*

What is the best thing about yourself? *"I love soccer."*

Christian wasn't just talking. Even as a kid, he understood that to be great at soccer, he couldn't just rely on his stronger foot. So when he practiced in his backyard, he worked on everything twice: 50 drills using his right foot, 50 drills using his left.

By the time he was 10, Christian was playing club soccer. He was so good that he often played with kids two years older than him. Christian wasn't scared. Playing against bigger kids helped him learn how to dribble faster and find space between defenders.

When he was 15, while representing the US under-17 national team, Christian scored a goal in the US's 4–1 victory over Brazil in an international friendly match. This was the moment he believed he could play soccer at the highest level—and maybe even become the greatest American soccer player in the world.

Christian's parents were very supportive of his dream. His dad took him to Europe during the summers to train and play in club matches. Just before Christian turned 16, he moved with his dad to Germany to play for Borussia Dortmund, a professional club in the Bundesliga, Germany's top league.

It was a huge opportunity but a risky move. Christian didn't know German, so he struggled to understand his teachers and the other kids at school. He also missed his friends and family back in the US. "That was the toughest year of my life by far," Christian said in an interview. "I just remember every day I thought, 'What am I doing here?'"

These struggles helped Christian become stronger. He kept training hard and trying to adapt to his new life in Germany. After thriving with the club's youth teams and winning the Under-19 Bundesliga title, Christian was promoted to Dortmund's senior team in 2016.

Just four months after joining the senior team,

Christian scored the first goal of his professional career in a 3-0 win against Hamburg. At 17 years old, he was the youngest non-German player to score a goal in Bundesliga history!

The following season, Christian set more records. He became Dortmund's youngest player to compete in the Champions League and the team's youngest scorer in the tournament when he scored in a match against Benfica.

That same season, Dortmund went all the way to the final of the DFB-Pokal, the German Cup. Christian was tripped up by an Eintracht Frankfurt player, winning a penalty. His teammate Pierre-Emerick Aubameyang scored the penalty, and Dortmund won their fourth German Cup in team history.

Christian's early success meant that people had even bigger expectations for him. But in the 2017-2018 season, Christian didn't do as well, and his team finished fourth in the league. Dortmund also changed coaches midway through the season, which didn't help Christian's growth.

International soccer was also challenging. Christian and the US Men's National Team (USMNT) lost to Trinidad and Tobago and failed to qualify for the 2018 World Cup. This was the first time in 32 years that the team hadn't qualified for the World Cup. It was a match considered by many as the most embarrassing one in American soccer history. For Christian, this was a bitter disappointment.

Christian needed a fresh start. He signed with Chelsea in the Premier League for the 2019–2020 season and had a great start. In a match against Burnley, Christian scored his first Premier League goals—and a perfect hat trick! This is when a player scores three goals in three different ways: one with their right foot, one with their left foot, and one with their head. At age 21, he was the youngest player in Chelsea history to record one.

In 2021, Christian also achieved one of his biggest dreams—winning the Champions League title. He scored Chelsea's only goal in the away semifinal against Real Madrid and assisted on the second goal in the home semifinal. Christian became the first American to play in—and win—a Champions League final!

But Christian also had to deal with changing coaches at Chelsea. Not all the coaches believed in Christian's abilities, choosing other players to start or play instead of him. Some coaches asked him to play in other positions that didn't feel as natural to him. It was hard for him to be a consistent player, and he kept getting hurt.

Christian needed another fresh start. So, in 2023, he transferred to AC Milan in Serie A, the Italian league. The team trusted him right away, and his coach made it clear that he would play often and at his preferred position. That support gave Christian confidence. In his first season, he delivered 12 goals and eight assists—his best year playing in Europe.

The following season, Christian helped lead AC Milan to a Supercoppa Italiana trophy. In the championship game, Christian scored the equalizer and assisted on the

game-winning goal. Christian was AC Milan's top scorer that season, with 17 goals and 10 assists.

Today, Christian is considered one of the greatest American soccer players of all time, as well as one of the world's most recognizable players. When he first left for Germany as a nervous teen, there weren't a lot of Americans playing in Europe. Now, many of the USMNT's stars play in Europe, and they thank Christian for paving the way for them.

Christian is just 27 years old, and he's not done with his soccer journey yet. He's also committed to paying it forward. He started the Christian Pulisic Legacy Program and partnered with Puma to set up community youth centers with soccer activity zones, camps, clinics, and more. "Captain America" is sure living up to his name!

ASISAT OSHOALA
OSHOALA
20

10

ASISAT OSHOALA

POSITION: Striker

BIRTH DATE: October 9, 1994

HOMETOWN: Ikorodu, Lagos State, Nigeria

TEAMS: FC Robo, Rivers Angels, Liverpool, Arsenal, Dalian Quanjian, FC Barcelona, Bay FC, Al Hilal

BREAKOUT MOMENT: In 2023, Asisat had an unbelievable six-match run with Barcelona, scoring a total of 12 goals, including three hat tricks. Her team won all six matches.

TOP ACHIEVEMENTS

- Six-time African Women's Footballer of the Year
- Two-time Women's Champions League winner
- Five-time La Liga winner
- 2021–2022 Pichichi Trophy winner (given to the top scorer in the Spanish league)
- First African woman to score in three consecutive Women's World Cups

DID YOU KNOW?

Growing up, Asisat wanted to be a lawyer but stuck with soccer after she realized she was so good at the sport.

In the 2023 Women's World Cup, striker Asisat Oshoala made history for her home country of Nigeria. She's got more than a million followers on social media, three Women's Champions League titles, five Spanish league titles, and six African Women's Footballer of the Year awards.

But all of it almost didn't happen, because her parents never wanted her to play.

Asisat grew up in Lagos, Nigeria, where she started playing soccer as a child just for fun on the streets. She loved soccer, but she didn't have dreams of becoming a professional. As one of 14 children, she helped support the family by selling peppers and other snacks on the streets.

Asisat's parents believed in the importance of doing well in school and having a quality education. Education was important to Asisat, but she couldn't deny her love for playing soccer. And the more she played, the more she realized she was good at it. But her parents did not support this idea.

"My parents didn't want me to play [soccer]. They didn't want me to do sports at all," Asisat said in an interview. "The mentality of the parents always for the girl-child is you're supposed to be at home—you're supposed to be helping your parents to cook or clean the house."

Asisat helped her parents cook and clean. But she also kept playing soccer with boys, as there were no other girls playing at the time. She snuck out of the house and played because she knew her parents wouldn't let her go if she asked.

Sometimes, her dad would drive past the field where she was playing. Her friends would warn her that her dad's car was about to pass by, and she would hide until his car was gone. Sometimes she would tell her parents she was going out to buy bread, which she did. But she wouldn't go home after that. She'd be on the field, playing soccer.

Asisat didn't always get away with keeping her secret from her parents. They had plenty

of arguments when it came to her playing soccer. The only relative who supported her was her grandmother. When her parents punished her by holding back food or money, her grandmother provided it. When Asisat didn't want to be home, her grandmother let her stay with her. With her grandmother's support, Asisat continued to play soccer.

When she was 15, Asisat was spotted by a scout while she was playing with some boys.

The scout contacted Emmanuel Osahon, the coach for professional women's club FC Robo. He said there was a player he might want to look at. Coach Osahon watched Asisat play and wanted her to join his team. This was an opportunity of a lifetime. Of course, Asisat wanted to join the team and play professionally.

But first, Coach Osahon needed to convince Asisat's parents. He was respectful of her parents' concerns, so he visited them in person. Coach Osahon told them that Asisat would be in good hands under his guidance. Her mom was still concerned, but her dad finally gave his blessing and allowed her to join the team.

This is when Asisat's life changed—not just for soccer, but for her family, too.

Playing with a professional team, she polished her skills and learned from her professional coaches. After a four-year run with Robo, Asisat played for Rivers Angels from 2013 to 2015, while also playing for the Nigerian national team. She was the highest goal scorer in the 2014 Under-20 Women's World Cup and named best player of the tournament. That same year, she helped Nigeria win the 2014 African Women's Championship. Best of all, Asisat's parents began supporting her soccer career and have been standing by her ever since.

From that point, Asisat's career took off. She went on a global tour, playing—and winning—with teams around the world. In 2016, as a member of English club Arsenal, Asisat won the 2016 FA Women's Cup. She then joined Chinese soccer club Dalian Quanjian, winning two league championships and a cup title.

Later playing for FC Barcelona in Spain, she helped the team win the 2019–2020 Copa de la Reina and Supercopa de España Femenina. And when Barcelona beat Chelsea in the 2020–2021 Champions League final,

Asisat became the first African woman to win a Champions League title.

Asisat's career reached icon status in Nigeria, as the first African woman to win Spain's Pichichi Trophy (given to the top goal scorer in the league). She was also nominated for the Ballon d'Or Féminin, given to the best female soccer player in the world each year.

But the best was about to come. During a group stage match in the 2023 Women's World Cup between Nigeria and Australia, Asisat came off the bench in the second half and volleyed the ball between an Australia defender and the goalie to score. After the goal, she took off her jersey (similar to Brandi Chastain in chapter 1!) and celebrated with her teammates.

Asisat's goal was a historic moment for her and her country. Nigeria defeated Australia in a 3–2 upset that day, shaking up the women's soccer world. The goal also made her the first African woman to score in three different

Women's World Cups. Her popularity around the world exploded!

Today, Asisat continues to play soccer professionally—currently with Al Hilal of the Saudi Women's Premier League. Back home, she is known as "Agba Baller," which means "legendary footballer." Off the pitch, she started the Asisat Oshoala Foundation, which helps empower young girls in Nigeria through sports, education, mentorship, and leadership development. Her mission now is to help give young girls the opportunities she didn't have herself.

Asisat's journey from challenge to champion reminds us that no dream is too big, no obstacle is too strong, and when you dare to chase your passion, you just might inspire a whole country.

VINÍCIUS "VINI" JUNIOR

11

VINÍCIUS "VINI" JUNIOR

POSITION: Left winger

BIRTH DATE: July 12, 2000

HOMETOWN: São Gonçalo, Brazil

TEAMS: Flamengo, Real Madrid

BREAKOUT MOMENT: Vini scored the only goal in the 2022 Champions League final as Real Madrid defeated Liverpool, 1-0. This victory was part of a huge turnaround season for Vini, who was thought of as an electrifying dribbler but could not score consistently.

TOP ACHIEVEMENTS

- Two-time Champions League winner
- Three-time La Liga champion
- 2023 La Liga Player of the Year
- 2024 Best FIFA Men's Player

DID YOU KNOW?

Vini is a huge basketball enthusiast. He's a big fan of LeBron James because of his athleticism, leadership, and activism off the court. Sometimes he even shows off with basketball-inspired goal celebrations, like pretending to shoot a basket.

Vinícius José Paixão de Oliveira Júnior, or Vini Junior, is one of soccer's biggest stars today. At only 25 years old, he's already arguably one of the best Real Madrid players ever.

On the pitch, Vini is one of the quickest and flashiest players out there. Fans love his dribbling skills and the creative ways he moves with the ball. Every time he scores, he celebrates with a fun dance. Kids try to imitate Vini when they play soccer, including his dance moves!

When you learn everything that Vini had to go through before becoming one of the world's best wingers, you'll appreciate his story even more.

Vini grew up in São Gonçalo, Brazil. His family was poor. They lived in a small house next to a busy highway, and his father worked many different jobs to put food on the table. Still, his parents were very supportive of Vini's dream of playing soccer.

When he was six years old, Vini started playing *futsal*, a faster indoor version of soccer. Played with a smaller ball, futsal relies on close ball control and quick passing. Thanks to playing futsal, Vini started to develop his quick feet and ability to dribble through tight spaces.

When Brazilian soccer club Flamengo saw how good of a futsal player Vini was, they invited him to join their youth academy. Vini's parents were willing to do anything to help their son chase his dreams. They borrowed money from a friend to pay for Vini to play at Flamengo—and agreed to clean the friend's house every weekend until the loan was paid off.

Their sacrifice paid off. Young Vini stood out from his first training session, impressing his coaches with his dribbling skills and blazing speed. He became an important player of Flamengo's "Generation 2000" team. They went undefeated for three straight years!

In 2015, Vini and Generation 2000 won the Copa Votorantim Sub-15, Brazil's oldest under-15 soccer tournament.

Vini also dazzled on the international stage. In 2017, he represented Brazil in the South American Under-17 Championship. Scoring seven goals in five matches, Vini led Brazil to the championship title! He was also named the tournament's best player and top scorer.

It didn't take long for the world to know the name Vini Junior. That same year, Vini played just 17 minutes in his first professional match with Flamengo before Real Madrid struck a deal for Vini to transfer to Real Madrid when he turned 18. One of the most famous soccer clubs in the world wanted Vini to play for them!

In 2018, Vini arrived at Real Madrid. He wasn't supposed to play much his first season since he was still very young. But when Cristiano Ronaldo left the team, Real Madrid needed Vini to play. Fans were excited to watch Vini, mesmerized by his quick play and amazing dribbling ability. They also loved that Vini always played with a smile.

Unfortunately, Vini struggled to score goals for Real Madrid. He scored just one goal in his first season before getting hurt. The next year, Vini had just three goals and three assists in La Liga, the Spanish league, that season. Things didn't improve much in the 2020-2021 season.

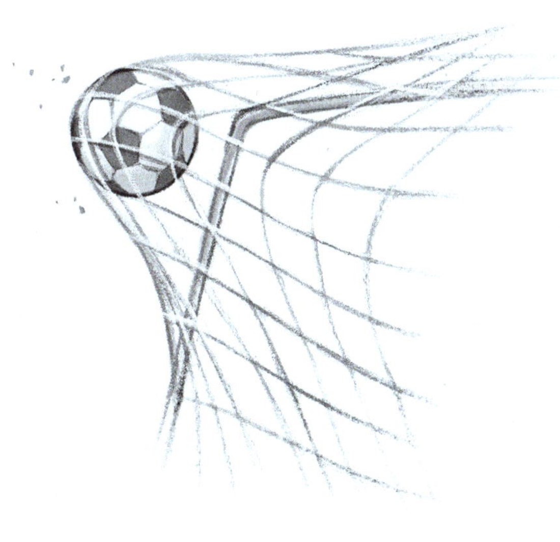

Teammates were getting frustrated with Vini's scoring slump—some even stopped passing the ball to him. He knew he had to get better. He started watching videos of himself playing to see what he was doing wrong. He realized that he needed to work on staying calm and focused in front of the goal.

He started watching film of some of his favorite goal scorers, too, to learn how they stayed calm and in control when approaching the net. He also worked with a psychologist to help prepare mentally for each match.

Vini started the 2021–2022 season on the bench. But when he entered the first match, he made an immediate impact, scoring a goal in a 4–1 win against Alavés. The next match, Vini came off the bench again and scored two goals to avoid defeat, leading Real Madrid to a 3–3 draw with Levante.

From there, Vini returned to the starting lineup. He scored 17 goals with 13 assists that season, bringing Real Madrid the La Liga title.

He didn't stop there. Real Madrid made it all the way to the Champions League final, where they defeated Liverpool, 1–0. That one goal? Scored by Vini!

Over the next few seasons Vini helped Real Madrid win two more La Liga titles and another Champions League title. In 2024, he earned the Best FIFA Men's Player Award.

Through all of his ups and downs, Vini has dealt with one other challenge: racism. He hears and sees it every time he's in another club's stadium: racist chants and gestures from opposing fans. Vini has asked for help from La Liga and other soccer organizations to address the issue, but not much has been done.

In Brazil, the Vinícius Jr. law was passed to combat racism in sporting events. The league has gotten a little better at punishing fans making racist chants, from being banned from the stadium to serving time in jail.

But guess what? None of this has stopped Vini from being on top of his game. He stays focused on winning for his team. In true champion spirit, he continues to play with joy and excitement. And when he scores, he continues to dance.

"I was a victim of xenophobia [dislike of people from other countries] and racism . . . but none of that started yesterday . . . the dances celebrate cultural diversity. Accept it, respect it. I won't stop," Vini posted on social media.

Back home in Brazil, he started the Instituto Vini Jr., running anti-racist education workshops for students. He also launched a campaign with the slogan, "Racism, don't pretend you don't see it." This slogan has appeared on posters and billboards all over major cities. He has won awards and honors for his efforts.

Vini's soccer story is still being written, and he has big dreams for both on and off the pitch. As Vini said in a 2025 interview: "I want to win more trophies with my club, win the most important competitions with the national team, and continue inspiring the next generation to believe in themselves."

ADA HEGERBERG

12

ADA HEGERBERG

POSITION: Striker

BIRTH DATE: July 10, 1995

HOMETOWN: Sunndalsøra, Norway

TEAMS: Kolbotn, Stabæk, Turbine Potsdam, Lyon

BREAKOUT MOMENT: Ada is the youngest player to score a hat trick in Toppserien, Norway's top division. Playing for Kolbotn, Ada was just 16 when she scored this game-winning hat trick!

TOP ACHIEVEMENTS

- Six-time Women's Champions League winner
- Eight-time Première Ligue champion
- 2018 Women's Ballon d'Or recipient
- 2016 UEFA Best Women's Player in Europe Award
- Two-time BBC Women's Footballer of the Year
- All-time scoring leader in the Women's Champions League

DID YOU KNOW?

Ada loves to read and is also a published author. She cowrote a book called *On the Same Team* with her soccer-playing sister, Andrine, and another author.

Norway's Ada Hegerberg is a goal-scoring machine and one of the best female soccer players in the world. She is the all-time leading scorer for Lyon of the Première Ligue, France's top soccer league for women. In one season, she scored 54 goals in just 35 matches. Her 66 goals in 62 matches is a record in the Women's Champions League. And she was the fastest player—male or female—to reach 50 goals in all of Champions League history. She needed just 49 matches to do it.

But if you're not familiar with who Ada Hegerberg is, you may be one of the many people who has never heard of her!

That's because even though she's popular in France and Norway, the rest of the world hasn't had many chances to watch her play. Why is that? Well, for five years, she stopped playing with Norway's national team. And her reason for staying away was far more important to her than winning matches and scoring goals.

To understand this, let's go back to Ada's childhood. She was born in a small village in Norway. Her parents were both soccer coaches, so you can say she was born into the sport. She was the youngest of three children, and her older brother and sister played soccer, too. In addition to soccer, they all talked about equality and that whether you're a boy or a girl, everyone should have the same opportunities.

Ada and her sister got involved in soccer by playing with boys. It didn't matter who won or lost. They all just loved being together and playing soccer. When Ada was 12, her family moved to Kolbotn, a town near Norway's capital city of Oslo. She got to join an all-girls team, but she noticed a difference in how girls were coached. Girls were expected to play cautiously and take everything slowly. Her coaches were quiet, and so were her teammates. They were not nearly as vocal as the ones she played with back home.

Soccer wasn't as exciting to play this way. This game is not meant to be played cautiously and slowly! Meanwhile, boys were encouraged to play with excitement and give it everything they had on the pitch.

Even at 12 years old, Ada knew this didn't make sense. Why were there specific rules for girls playing soccer, and why were they being treated differently than the boys when they played?

When she was 16, Ada became a professional. Her first club was with Kolbotn of the Toppserien League, the top professional league in Norway. She made an immediate impact with the team. In her first season, she became the youngest player in team and league history to score a hat trick. She ended the season as the team's top scorer and was voted the league's Young Player of the Year.

A year later, Ada joined her sister and began playing for Stabæk, another club in the same league. In one game, she scored five goals in just the first half! That season, she was Toppserien's highest scorer, with 25 goals in just 18 matches.

She went on to play for one season in Germany with Turbine Potsdam, then moved to France in 2014 to play for Lyon. Here, she achieved the most success in her professional career. She scored 26 goals in 22 league matches her first year. And she won the first of six Première Ligue championships in a row.

Lyon was also a frequent participant in the Champions League, and Ada helped the team win a record five Champions League titles in a row. When the Ballon d'Or Féminin award was created in 2018 for the game's top female soccer player, Ada became the first player to receive it.

Still, something was bothering Ada. Even though she was successful as a professional, she didn't like how women's soccer was being treated, particularly in her home country of Norway. There, women's soccer didn't receive the same kind of money, resources, or respect that men's soccer received.

Ada never stopped questioning why female players were treated differently than male players. In fact, she loved playing for Lyon because they treated their male and female players equally. But she didn't see the same progress from Norway's national team. So, in 2017, Ada decided to stop playing for her country. This meant missing the 2019 Women's World Cup, where the rest of the world could have seen her play.

"We live in a world where equality is the most important thing," Ada once said in an interview. "Women must have their spots, and that's in society."

For five years, Ada, Norway's best player, chose not to represent her country. Finally, a change was made in the Norwegian Football Federation leadership. The federation improved travel, equipment, and facilities for the women's team. And they gave the men's and women's national teams equal pay.

Ada decided to return to Norway's national team in 2022. In her first game back, she scored a hat trick against Kosovo in a World Cup qualifying match, which Norway won.

On the pitch, Ada continues to be a leader for Lyon and for Norway's national team. Off the pitch, she's working to make a difference for women's soccer. She knows there is still more work to be done when it comes to equality in the sport. But she believes that her willingness to sacrifice her own career to help future female soccer players was worth the effort.

"Give the women and the girls the same opportunity to do their sports . . ." she said. "That's what I've been saying for a lot of years now, but it won't change by itself; you need to push for it."

Post-Game Notes

By reading these 12 stories, you can see what it took for these players and teams to become champions. It didn't come easily for any of them, right? I hope you've found many lessons in these stories that inspire you.

The 1999 US Women's National Team and Leicester City showed that success can come from hard work, teamwork, and trusting one another. These two teams faced different expectations, but they both had the same approach to becoming champions.

Sadio Mané, Mo Salah, and Christian Pulisic showed that there can be bumps on the road to becoming a champion. They knew that just because they were not as successful playing for one team, that didn't make them bad at playing soccer. Failure was not the end for them—it was just part of the process. This is what Sadio, Mo, and Christian learned when they worked through their challenges and found success with their new teams.

The stories of Alex Morgan, Marta, and Asisat Oshoala prove that you can be great at something even if someone else says you're not or that you shouldn't even try. These three had pure love for the game and decided that they wouldn't let anything or anyone get in the way of playing a sport that brings them joy.

Gigi Buffon taught us that even great success doesn't always bring total happiness. It's brave to ask for help so you can get back to a better place while doing what you love.

Likewise, David Clarke and Lionel Messi show us that physical differences don't have to get in the way of reaching great heights, breaking records, or just doing what you love.

The stories of Vini Junior and Ada Hegerberg remind us that even world champions run into obstacles and injustices. They show us how we can all make a difference through our words and actions to help others, like they do against racism and inequality.

Now that you've read about these players and teams, how did their stories inspire you? Ask yourself:

- Which of these stories affected me the most, and why?
- What am I most passionate about?
- Is there anything that is keeping me from following my passion?
- What can I do to take the first step in making my dreams a reality?
- What's a challenge I overcame? What did I learn from that experience?

Whether your dream is soccer or another passion, I hope you find inspiration from these stories that can help you grow from challenge to champion!

12 More Soccer Stars to Know

The 12 stories you read are just some of the many inspiring soccer stories. Here are a dozen more players you can follow.

TYLER ADAMS (MIDFIELDER)

Considered one of the top American players in the game today, Tyler Adams is a homegrown player of the New York Red Bulls Academy. When he was 12, he signed with the Red Bulls under-13 team and moved up to the reserve team when he was 16. As a single parent, his mom made many sacrifices to support Tyler, driving 150 miles roundtrip several times a week to take him to practice. She remarried, and Tyler gained a dad and three new brothers who loved soccer as much as he did!

His mom's sacrifices and his family's support paid off as Tyler worked his way up to the top of the Red Bulls ranks. Internationally, he helped the US Men's National Team win two CONCACAF Nations League titles. He captained the national team at the 2022 World Cup and was named US Soccer Male Player of the Year. As of 2025, Tyler plays for Bournemouth of the Premier League.

BARBRA BANDA (STRIKER)

One of the best female players in the game today, Barbra Banda was captain of Zambia's national team in the 2020 and 2024 Olympics and became Africa's all-time leading scorer in Olympic soccer history.

While growing up, Barbra was encouraged to play soccer by her father, who also played. However, her mother disapproved. Her school didn't have a girls' team, so she played with the boys. At age 14, she joined the under-17 Women's National Team. She soon became the first Zambian soccer player to play in Europe, with Spanish club EDF Logroño. From there, she moved to China to play for Shanghai Shengli. Barbra joined the NWSL's Orlando Pride in 2024, where she led the team to win the NWSL championship and was named league MVP.

Barbra's mother is now her number one fan. Although Barbra's father passed away when she was 16, she continues to dedicate her success to him.

AITANA BONMATÍ (MIDFIELDER)

Considered one of the world's best female soccer players, Aitana Bonmatí is a three-time Ballon d'Or award winner and 2024 FIFA Best Women's Player.

As a child, Aitana was the only girl on her team because not many girls played soccer. Eventually, she was no longer allowed to play on the boys' team, but luckily, FC Barcelona saw her talent and invited her to play for them. She's played for Barcelona since 2016 and has six Liga F titles under her belt, along with three Champions League titles. She also won the 2023 Women's World Cup as a member of Spain's women's national team.

Even though she's a fierce competitor, she admits that she sometimes doesn't feel confident in herself. She started seeing a psychologist when she was 13. Today, she speaks openly about the importance of mental health and getting help when needed.

OUSMANE DEMBÉLÉ (STRIKER)

As a young boy, Ousmane Dembélé always had a ball at his feet, and he was talented! Coaches couldn't believe their eyes, calling his dribbling skills "insane." Scouts all wanted him on their teams.

Today, Ousmane is a double threat on the pitch, as he can shoot, pass, and dribble with either foot, making him twice as challenging to defend. As a member of France's national team, Ousmane won the World Cup in 2018. He's won three La Liga titles with FC

Barcelona, along with two Copa del Rey titles and two Supercopas de España.

But you can say he's now at the top of his game after leading Paris Saint-Germain to a Ligue Un championship and a Champions League title. As the 2025 Ballon d'Or winner, Ousmane is one of just 10 players to have won a World Cup, a Champions League title, and the Ballon d'Or.

EBERECHI EZE (MIDFIELDER)

Eberechi Eze thought his career was over before he was even 20 years old. Born in London to Nigerian parents, Eberechi dreamed of playing for Arsenal. His dream came true when the team signed him at 8 years old, but they released him when he was 13. He also played for (and was released by) Fulham, Reading, and Millwall. Eberechi thought his soccer career had ended, and he was only 18. He thought about quitting. But then Queens Park Rangers took a chance on him.

Eberechi worked hard to become a better soccer player and believe in himself. He moved on to play for Crystal Palace, where he helped lead the team to the 2025 FA Cup—Crystal Palace's first trophy in team history. Today, Eberechi is back with his dream team of Arsenal as one of the best players in England. And to think he almost quit!

NAOMI GIRMA (DEFENDER)

Growing up in California as the child of Ethiopian immigrants, Naomi Girma played soccer for fun with friends from the Ethiopian community. None of their parents thought the games were more than just fun bonding activities. But Naomi had other plans.

After playing some club soccer, Naomi was recruited to play for Stanford University. As one of the best college defenders, Naomi was selected as the number one pick in the 2022 NWSL Draft by the San Diego Wave. There, she won Rookie of the Year and Defender of the Year.

The following year, she became the first defender to be named as US Soccer Female Player of the Year. On the US Women's National Team, Naomi was the only player to play every single minute in the 2024 Summer Olympics. As of 2025, Naomi plays for Chelsea in the Women's Super League.

HANNAH HAMPTON (GOALKEEPER)

Even British royalty has noticed Hannah Hampton, winner of the 2025 Women's Yashin Trophy, given to the best female goalkeeper in the world. In the 2024–2025 season with Chelsea, her 13 clean sheets tied for the most in a single Women's Super League season. She helped Chelsea capture the Women's Super League title, FA Cup, and League Cup, becoming the first Chelsea goalie to do so.

Pretty amazing, especially for someone with vision challenges! Hannah was born with an eye condition that causes blurred vision and difficulty with judging distances. Although

Hannah has had operations to try to correct her condition, she still deals with the effects. But she's discovered strategies for dealing with fast-moving soccer balls shot toward her net.

As for her connections to the royal family, Hannah was honored in 2025 by the Duchess of Edinburgh for her efforts to raise awareness about eye health.

SON HEUNG-MIN (STRIKER)

Son Heung-Min's training to become a great soccer player was more military style than traditional style. Son's father, a former pro soccer player, trained him and his brother for six hours a day!

When Son was 16, he moved from South Korea to Germany to play soccer. He didn't understand the language and missed his mom's cooking. He described those years as "painful" but never told his parents. He also dealt with racism and doubts about his abilities. But Son kept working hard and let his performances on the pitch do the talking.

Son moved to England in 2015, where he became a key player for Tottenham Hotspur. He later became captain and led the team to win the Europa League in 2025. That same year, he joined Los Angeles FC of MLS.

Son has adjusted well, connected with his teammates and fans, and even threw out the first pitch at a Los Angeles Dodgers baseball game!

PEDRI (MIDFIELDER)

Pedro González López, known as Pedri, is a young talent from the Canary Islands who soccer fans should keep an eye on. At 23 years old, Pedri plays like a seasoned veteran. On the pitch, he's calm under pressure. When he has the ball, he hardly ever loses possession, and he's great at dribbling his way out of tight spaces.

With FC Barcelona, Pedri has won two La Liga titles, two Copa del Rey championships, and two Supercopas de España. In 2021, he received the Kopa Trophy and Golden Boy award as the best soccer player under 21 years old. Pedri helped Spain's national team capture the 2023 UEFA Nations League title and the 2024 European Championship.

Pedri is a born athlete, but he also took his schoolwork seriously, even receiving a scholarship to study medicine. For now, though, watch for him on the pitch!

TRINITY RODMAN (FORWARD)

Trinity Rodman may be the daughter of NBA champion Dennis Rodman, but she's carving out a legacy of her own in the soccer world. Trinity started playing club soccer when she was 10, encouraged by her mother and role model, Michelle, who raised Trinity and her brother as a single parent.

Trinity won four national titles for the

So Cal Blues soccer club. Though she committed to play college soccer at UCLA, Trinity never played there due to the COVID-19 pandemic. Instead, she turned pro and was selected second overall by the Washington Spirit of the NWSL.

As of 2025, Trinity is still the youngest player ever to be drafted in the NWSL. Washington made an excellent choice: She helped them win the 2021 NWSL title and was named 2021 Rookie of the Year. In 2024, she helped the US Women's National Team win the Olympic gold medal. Keep watching!

VIRGIL VAN DIJK (DEFENDER)

Standing at six foot five, Virgil van Dijk of the Netherlands has the size, strength, and ability to jump high that make him one of the best central defenders today. For the entire 2018-2019 Premier League season, not a single opposing player was able to successfully dribble past him.

As a teen, though, his odds didn't look good. He admits he was slow. He wasn't considered a standout player, and his club didn't see a contract in his future. But he kept playing and grew taller and was eventually scouted for Dutch football club FC Groningen, where he became a key player.

Now with Liverpool, the Dutch defender has won two Premier League titles, a Champions League title, the FA Cup, and the Community Shield. In 2019, he was runner-up for the Ballon d'Or. Internationally, Virgil has played in more than 80 matches for the Netherlands' national team and was named team captain for the 2026 World Cup.

LAMINE YAMAL (WINGER)

When Lamine Yamal was a baby, his family won a contest to be in a photo shoot. A photo from the shoot, which appeared in a charity calendar, shows little Lamine in a bathtub, being visited by none other than Lionel Messi!

The young FC Barcelona winger has a mature understanding of the game and advanced dribbling skills. Lamine is a player who can make quick plays based on what he's seeing.

With FC Barcelona, he's already won two La Liga titles, a Copa del Rey title, and a Supercopa de España title. He starred at the 2024 UEFA European Championship with Spain, becoming the youngest player to play in—and win—the tournament. Lamine has earned the Kopa Trophy twice, as well as a Golden Boy award. He even came in second for the 2025 Ballon d'Or!

Considered one of the most exciting young stars in all of soccer, Lamine will represent Spain's national team at the 2026 World Cup. His story is still being written!

Acknowledgments

I couldn't have written about the "beautiful game" without a beautiful set of people who inspire me.

To my wife, Sandy Navalta. Your love and support keeps me going, even during the toughest times. Thank you for being you. To my family—Pati Navalta, Cicero Estrella, Ludy Navalta, and Julie Poblete. I love you and I hope I've made you all proud.

A special shoutout to Tim Cummins, probably the biggest Arsenal fan I'll ever know. Thank you for always being willing to talk soccer with me, and for reminding me that the FA Cup is a very meaningful trophy.

I also want to acknowledge my father, Glorino "Lory" Navalta, who was a great writer and introduced me to sports. I miss watching games with you, Dad. But I thank you for passing your gift along to me and allowing me to tell stories to future generations.

About the Author

Born and raised in the San Francisco Bay Area, **Chris Navalta** studied journalism at Sacramento State University. As a sports reporter, he covered high school and college sports such as football, basketball, baseball, and soccer. After his days as a journalist, Chris began working in sports public relations with NBA teams (Sacramento Kings and Golden State Warriors) and in Minor League Baseball (Sacramento River Cats).

Chris's first book with Zeitgeist, *Basketball Stars: Stories and Skills from the NBA's and WNBA's Best Players*, was published in 2025. Today, Chris leads award-nominated PR campaigns in the video game industry. He continues to work with athletes, connecting them with their favorite video games.

About the Illustrator

Lorenzo Fornaciari is an illustrator, graphic designer, and teacher. He has loved drawing his whole life, and after attending Scuola Internazionale di Comics in Reggio Emilia, Italy, he began work as a freelance illustrator. He has lived in the UK and Italy while creating illustrations for children's books, and was a teacher of storyboarding and Photoshop at Scuola Internazionale di Comics. He has worked on many exciting projects, from video games and animation to websites, comics, and board games.

Hi, parents and caregivers,

We hope your child enjoyed *Inspiring Stories of Soccer Greats*. If you have any questions or concerns about this book, or have received a damaged copy, please contact customerservice@penguinrandomhouse.com. We're here and happy to help.

Also, please consider writing a review on your favorite retailer's website to let others know what you and your child thought of the book!

Sincerely,

The Zeitgeist Team

SCORE THE REST OF THE BOOKS IN THE

SERIES!

"From overcoming challenges to advocating for change, *From Challenge to Champion* shows how true champions inspire us both on and off the field."

—ALLYSON FELIX, seven-time Olympic gold medalist and founder of Saysh

Stories of top athletes like Simone Biles, Serena Williams, Tom Brady, LeBron James, and others highlight the power of hard work and perseverance.

Featuring NFL stars like Saquon Barkley, Josh Allen, and Jerry Rice, read about the challenges these athletes have overcome on their path to triumph.

Shohei Ohtani. Aaron Judge. Reggie Jackson. Hank Aaron. What do they share? Resilience and the drive to win! Read about top MLB players in this fun and fact-packed book.

Parents and caregivers can learn more about these books and upcoming titles at **zeitgeistpublishing.com**